This Book is presented

To

_____

By

_____

On This Day

_____

VISIONS *of* REALITY

Volume II

PRINCE L. WHITMORE, SR.

authorHOUSE®

AuthorHouse™
1663 Liberty Drive
Bloomington, IN 47403
www.authorhouse.com
Phone: 1 (800) 839-8640

Published by AuthorHouse 12/29/2017

ISBN: 978-1-5462-1978-1 (sc)
ISBN: 978-1-5462-1977-4 (e)

Library of Congress Control Number: 2017919408

Print information available on the last page.

This book is printed on acid-free paper.

Scripture quotations marked KJV are from the Holy Bible, King James Version
(Authorized Version). First published in 1611. Quoted from the KJV Classic
Reference Bible, Copyright © 1983 by The Zondervan Corporation.

Dedication

To my mother and sister,
The late Dorothy Whitmore and Donna Baker
who were "Inspirations" for
the troubled soul.

Acknowledgments

I acknowledge all the people who have touched my life with emotional tie that generated the creation of my writing. I am forever indebted to my loving wife, Barbara, and children, ReKeshia, Prince II and Franchesca for excusing me from family time in order to devote it to the writing of this book. I also thank Marques Hendrix for being so willing to read and make valuable comments on the manuscript.

Special consideration goes to Jimmy and Nanthalia McJamerson for their encouragement and motivation on this manuscript. Alfred Twymon, Sylvia Reese and James Flowers are highly appreciated for critiquing the manuscript. I am appreciative to Terrell Robinson for adding spice to the manuscript through illustrations. It is also with indebtedness I owe Nita Thomas and Evelyn Dukes for the countless hours they spent with typing the work. I am grateful to Emily Winston and Wanda Gray for dreaming with me and seeing the finish product before it actually happened. I would further like to acknowledge and thank my sister, Maretta W. Henderson for her countless hours of typing and proofreading on this edition of Visions of Reality, Volume 2.

All praises to God for His will in causing this book to be finished.

Contents

Foreword

Each life is given moments of bliss as well as tranquility that come from just being a part of this vast universe. One knows that in order to exist, each positive must have a negative. Life always balances the scale of joy and ecstasy with the weight of pain and sorrow.

The second of two volumes titled Visions of Reality is a mixture of joy and happiness mingled with the pain and sorrows that I conveyed as making life meaningful and rewarding. My visions of what life can be, as opposed to actuality, encourage the reader to maintain hope and assurance in trusting a higher being, God, to comfort and sustain during their darkest hour. Through the reading of these poems, the reader will gain a quest for understanding love while not rejecting disparity.

Introduction

"If I could just find the words!" We often say to ourselves as we struggle to express pain or to exhibit joy. We long for the language to get the feelings out to share them to eject them from our bodies or souls. But, often we cannot access those expressions until a poet comes along and utters the words for us. Then, and only then, we are free. Thank you, Prince Whitmore, for being such a poet.

Prince Whitmore is a modest man who probably has no idea how urgent, how important, how piercing, powerful and beautiful his work is. We are grateful for his generosity of sharing his work through this collection.

During the twenty years I have known Mr. Whitmore, he has been devoted to truth and healing. Those values are shown in his poetry. Although he is focused and "contained" he is not narrow. His work gives a clear indication of his breadth: from strength to vulnerability, from work to play, from life to death, from worship of God to adoration of his wife.

This book-powerhouse of wisdom and love-contains sections. Spiritual Guidance is filled with poems of hope. No matter how heavy your burdens, hope "springs back" into your heart because Mr. Whitmore gives us instructions and encouragement concerning our part and God's possibilities in handling life's problems.

The second part of the book, Toils of Love, was given an appropriate title, as it expresses much of the sadness, sensitivity, loss and pain involved in loving others. Life in general, often involves pain and struggles as noted in the "Toils of Life" section. We are not left in pain, however, as Mr. Whitmore provide the contrasting, glorious, sensual, and beautiful sides of love in the "Marriage" section of this collection.

You may need to brace yourself for the "Ethics" section of this book. We are admonished to straighten up, strengthen up and soften up on others as our character is built or refined with these poems.

The "Dad" section is difficult to read, but absolutely necessary in the hundreds of cases which apply. There is scathing indictment within these words as well as timely challenges as families enter the new millennium.

Finally, the universal blessing called "Friendship" is celebrated at the end of the poetry collection. It is clear that this simple concept has far- reaching impact on the world.

Thank you, Mr. Whitmore, for sharing your talent as one of God's messengers!

Nanthalia W. McJamerson, Ph. D.
Grambling State University

Part I

Religion

I am the door: by me if any man enter in, he shall be saved and shall go in and out, and find pasture.

St. John 10:9

If It Seems Your Life's A Mess

If it seems your life's a mess –
Even though you've done your best,
Then allow God to do his part
For he can lighten your troubled heart.

If it seems your life's a mess -
Can't manage to pass it's golden test;
Then let the savior be your guide-
All your needs he will provide.

If it seems your life's a mess
Can't even gain a little success,
Try opening up to God in prayer,
And you will find He will always be there.

If it seems your life's a mess
Having trouble in making progress,
Then tell God of your misery and pain
And cock your trigger but let Him aim.

God is the key to what we Need,
If only His words we would heed;
If it seems your life's a mess,
Turn to the Father for He's the best.

I Needed God

I searched the world for fame and glory
Only to find my life a meaningless story,
Wearied and depressed-I kneeled and sobbed;
Was then I found I needed God.

I searched for love to ease my mind,
Went to great length to have a good time;
But couldn't see my joys were robbed
Because I failed to realize I needed God.

I tried drugs to relax my soul
But still felt lonely and my world seemed cold.
I gained worldly riches and a prestigious job
Yet there stood misery for I needed God.

Through all my trying to live without care
No matter where I turned my conscience was there;
It whipped my ego and made me a slob
For rejecting the thought that I needed God.

"This Too Shall Pass Away"

When lonely and in need of tender loving care
and your friends you thought were many seem no longer there;
When depressed and upset because man led you astray-
In the Bible is the saying, "This too shall pass away."

When the pressures of the world seem to fall down on you
And you cry out for relief but nothing seems to do;
If frustrated and confused about the worldly problems today-
In the Bible is the saying, "This too shall pass away."

While on the road of success-reaching for brighter skies;
The higher you climb the mountain,
the more you're confronted with lies.
Now in bed you toss and turn because of problems of the day;
In the Bible is the saying, "This too shall pass away."

When the future looks very dim-not a speck of hope in sight,
and your mind is fogged with fears from the darkness of the night;
Filled with prejudice and pains-this dreary world we stay;
In the Bible is the saying, "This too shall pass away."

My Savior Reigns

Life for me has come to an end
on this side of the troubled shore.
I go to a place where peace abounds-
worries plaguing my soul no more.
The road I trod was often paved
with the mixtures of despair and pain.
This path has led me to the other side-
the place where my Savior reigns.

Glory land, oh glory land-
I marvel at your sight.
I kept the faith for I knew one day
I would behold God's marvelous light.
Even though at times the pressures of life
were about to drive me insane,
there was no doubt at journey's end,
I would dwell where my Savior reigns.

It's not that I have gone away
to a distant, foreign land.
I've just gone home after completing my course,
which was designed in the Master's plan.
Nothing can compare to what I'm feeling
in this dwelling that I now can claim.
Rejoice on my moving to a better place-
I'm where my Savior reigns.

Be Of Good Cheer

It's rather painful when we make a mistake
But Christ paid the price when nailed to the stake,
He gave His all before earth he departed
So no one would have to live down-hearted.

If you have a need Christ is there
But you must first show that you care
By falling down on your knees and pray
To give you strength and show you the way.

He loves you so much that He gave His life
Which is to all the supreme sacrifice,
So you know He's with you to the end
Not to condemn but to be your friend.

God loves and will provide your needs
If His words you strive to heed,
So trust Him for He is always near
Wanting you to be of good cheer.

To Receive the Proper Pay

Each life that carries the breath of God
and confesses in Jesus name,
Is given the time to accomplish a job-
which no man has the same.
And unto each there's a season-
a period for a resting day,
when the Heavenly Father will call his own
to receive the proper pay.

It matters not the length of time
for your job to be completed,
For all are given a task
that just can't be deleted;
But then there comes the Angel of God
descending from Heaven to say
"Come home little sheep, come home,
to receive the proper pay."

God wouldn't let us labor
if he had no reward;
Neither would he promise an eternal home
just to keep us looking forward.
We all are of God's Kingdom
when we serve him every day,
And he relieves us from our toils and strife
to receive the proper pay.

"If Only You Knew What I Know"

Even though this day seems sad
for the friends I'm leaving behind,
I'm going to a better place-
free at last of mourning and crying.
There is no pain and suffering
nor sorrows on my face to show,
I'm safe in my Father's precious care-
If only you knew what I know.

"I go to prepare a place,"
are the words my savior said.
I'm just beginning to live-
though the world thinks I'm dead.
The joy is beyond compare
and there's love wherever I go.
Fret not that I have departed;
If only you knew what I know.

Heaven's gates will open wide
to receive my soul at last.
I finished the course set before me,
though uneasy sometimes was my task.
"In my Father's house are many mansions"
and His light is a radiant glow.
"Earth has no sorrows that Heaven can't heal."
If only you knew what I know.

Part II

Toils of Love

How Much Longer

How much longer will it be
Before you confess you've stopped loving me;
The emptiness in your eyes does say
That your love is going away.

How much longer can you hide
The vacancy of a love that's died;
Is it another your heart desires-
And is it you he too admires?

How much longer will you hold on
Because you feel leaving is wrong,
Refusing to obey the voice inside;
Afraid to trust your heart as guide.

It's so important to thyself be true,
Which will create a happier you.
When we caress I feel the change,
And how much longer before I feel the pain.

Nothing Left

This life we live as time passes on
Has been so right yet been so wrong.
We thought of each other by thinking of self
And took until love had nothing left.

I wanted my way to give to you
But in return you did so too.
We fought to rule by selfish desire,
Now nothing's left of our empire.

Times have been sweet to be so bitter;
Where once stood love's giants-we now are little.
We now realize when love is gone
There can be no foundation to strengthen a home.

We gave our all but in return
We sought more than we had earned.
Now for life we keep on giving
With nothing left to keep love living.

So Alone

Desperately searching
to find peace within my soul-
I bandaged the pain
with lawless pleasure.
The torture of rejection
mingled with denial
only enhanced my defects
another measure.

Life's deficiencies and blemishes
creating a phantom
that can stifle the gallant
without hesitation,
entangled in traps
of false craved security,
which leads
to my ultimate termination.

Surrounded by objects-
once beautiful to behold,
simply adds emptiness
to a desecrated soul.
Possessing wealth of the world-
Now I shall be strong,
Engulfed by friends-
nevertheless so alone.

"A Lonely Love"

When I think of your cherry lips and
how your smile does shine,
It's then I sat so lonesome-hearted,
realizing you're not mine.
Oh how I wanted my thought of you
to be of a true loyal friend,
but in lonesomeness I find myself,
for my desires for you won't end.

I tell myself that thoughts of you
will somehow soon be gone,
But in my heart I find each thought
someway lingers on.
I can fool the world about the way I feel
but to myself I can't pretend.
I crave too hard for your gentle touch
yet knowing I just can't win.

I know you strive to be true to your spouse
and I will love only my wife;
Yet without your touch and warm embraces
incompleteness is the story of my life.
I need to know that you care for me,
that-my needing you isn't in vain;
But even if you didn't care for me,
my love for you would remain.

I now feel weak but if you care
don't let me under your skin,
For the beauty you show would be no more
if your love I could somehow win.
We both must love only our mates
and let each other be;
And though I live in need of you
I couldn't stand you needing me.

Forbidden Happiness

The sleep that made me lie awake
ere my eyes came open
Was of a joy, tranquility-
of words not to be spoken.
The pleasure, thrill and ecstasy
upon me calm and bliss,
produced the fruit of inward lust-
forbidden happiness.

How I crave to hold you close,
to squeeze, to feel, to embrace
Your tender body upon my body,
your shyness to erase.
Now whilst my hunger for you grows
with such an unquenchable quest,
Tis but the fruit of your crop
Yields forbidden happiness.

In my heart my hunger grows
Yet knowing it can't be fed,
I drop my head in silence,
This lust so tenaciously I dread.
I can't control my cravings of beauty,
My desires for your touch as my guest;
Yet in truth of reality
You're forbidden happiness.

Your Friend

Should I strive to be your friend
when I know all along
I want to be more
than what I have shown,
I want to give more
than what I can give
I want to do more
each day that I live.

Should I strive to be your friend
though deep in my heart
There always lingers emptiness
whenever we are apart,
There's always something missing
even when a crowd is near
That can easily be found
the second you appear.

Should I strive to be your friend
for you to have when in need
When I know that such a friendship
is the start of selfish greed,
when I know I wouldn't rest
until your heart was a part of mine,
When I know I can't be yours
and you could never be mine.

Part III

Ethics

Let not the foot of pride come against me, and let not the hand of the wicked remove me.

Psalms 36:11

Does It Help To Complain

When you speak of the way things are,
Does your speech go very far,
Or does it linger with bitter disdain;
Tell me please, does it help to complain?

When you say a law is not fair
Would you change it or would you dare
Risk your job to achieve this aim;
Again I ask, does it help to complain?

When you speak of how children fuss
Did it occur to you that their teachers are us,
Living so wildly but wanting the children tamed;
They do as we do so does it help to complain?

Can you see the world at peace-
A place where man will dwell with wild beasts;
If so, why complain of moral decay,
For as predicted, it will all pass away.

When you speak of being treated wrong,
Did it occur to you that it makes you strong,
For each mountain you climb that's in your way
Will make you even stronger the following day.

Meditate on how you live your life;
Is it free from sin and earthly vice,
Or is it like others with a little touch of shame
Who just like you have no right to complain.

"Step By Step"

Life can only give
The things you make appear,
Which comes about
Through diligent efforts
and the will-
to continue.

The road you travel
will be rugged;
You possess the power
To mold it-into a mountain
or pit.
Stay on the right trail
Or you may forever be lost.

Never forget your past,
it guides your steps-
For the future.
You are your Master
But without God-
You are a slave.

You have moved
Up the ladder
With zeal and success.
Continue striving
Step by Step
And you will reach
the top.

The Lustful Man In Me

The desires in me that's beyond my control
Are making me weak, mean and cold,
It's a battle for strength to be set free
And kill my enemy-the lustful man in me.

"If thou right eye offend, then pluck it out,"
Maybe it takes blindness to win this bout
And yet in the mind lust would prevail
Sending me eternally to a fiery hell.

What if I lived my heart's desire
Making this world my golden empire,
But all is vain in beauty and lust
At the day of judgement when returned to dust.

Never give in to defeat when fighting a wrong
Will be my philosophy-my everyday song;
The battle will continue through pain and misery
Until I'm the victor over the lustful man in me.

Cast the First Stone

When it seems there's no hope
For the life you live today
And all you see are mistakes
And the price for them you must pay;
There's one good consolation-
God forgives for our wrong
And reminds those who judge
"He who's without sin cast the first stone."

When it seems there's no tomorrow
Due to errors of your past
And you drown in your sorrow-
Thinking your future is as shattered glass,
Just remember God will provide
And will strengthen in time of need
And reassures He's by your side
When His words you strive to heed.

When it seems your world is crumbling
For things didn't turn out right
And you continue slipping and fumbling
In such of a guiding light,
God has been there from the start
But allows you to move on your own
And because of His love He warn others
"He who's without sin cast the first stone."

God is wanting you, his child
To come to him in secret prayer,
He can comfort and place a smile
Where now linger chaos and despair,
He still loves and has the power
To be your friend when you feel alone
And lets you know no man is perfect for
"He who's without sin cast the first stone."

It's Up To You

It's up to you if you're to win
And not the color of your ebony skin,
You hold the key to the success you would like
Regardless of the fact that your race is black.

It's up to you to gain a crown
Though the world tries to bring you down,
And when it seems it's on your back
Don't start regretting that your race is black.

It's up to you to reach the top
Though sometimes you want to stop;
Just keep on reaching for the sky
And soon you'll obtain your heart's desire.

There's joy in knowing that we are free
With control over our destiny;
It matters not what you say or do
Whether you succeed or fail-it's up to you.

I Tried to Cry Today

I tried to cry today
but the tears would not appear.
Regardless of how I sighed and moaned
no mist would linger near.
The plight of the world grieved me
as I beheld its moral decay.
The bridge that once crossed the river Pride
has somehow crumbled away.

I tried to cry today
as I beheld pain on the faces
of those who longed for peace on earth
and unity of all races.
It's a shame we've come so far
yet still can't figure out
the way to joy is not through violence
nor is it through wealth no doubt.

Will we ever really love
and share our overflow
to help a friend who has a need
or aid a stranger we may not know?
It's time we make a change
and seek a better way.
When will the bitterness come to an end?
I tried to cry today.

Part IV

Dad

What Would Say?

Yesteryears when I was young
I asked you if I was your son,
You said to me "there could be no way;
I was nowhere around that day."

Times have changed and I am grown,
I'm out there all on my own;
Knowing I need no handout today
If I asked now, what would you say?

Would you be ashamed to confess
As a father to me you failed the test,
Just didn't need another son in your life
For you already had other children and a wife.

You constantly remained on my mind
And probably will until the end of time,
So if I asked that question today,
With a truthful heart, what would you say?

Our Father which art in heaven, Hallowed be they name.

St. Matthew 6:9

Most men will proclaim everyone his own
goodness; but a faithful man who can find?

Proverbs 20:6

Happy Father's Day

I have a feeling for you
That's so hard to define,
Although I know you disown me
I still feel you are mine.

You are that special man
Who played an important part,
For without the seed you planted
I could never have made a start.

Yes, you are my dad,
I can feel it in my heart.
Although you still may hate me-
I loved you from the start.

Dad

When I was a tiny lad
I often wondered-who was my dad?
I knew mother's footsteps before her face she would show
But where was dad- I wanted to know.

As my friends chatted of things their fathers said
All I could do was drop my head;
Since I knew not dad-what could I say,
With drooped head, I walked slowly away.

As I grew older, I learned dad's name,
I was told of his style and of his game,
How he had children scattered all around,
Some say he has children in every town.

Now I see why dad never came to say
"Hello my son-I'm proud of you today."
He didn't have time to waste on me-
He had too many other children to see.

Now I am a man and dad is old,
And for some reason to me, he's a precious old soul;
Even though he never said "how is my lad"
I can't help but love him because dad is dad.

Since dad wasn't there when I needed him most
I find in life-my dad is a ghost;
A figment of my imagination that could never be-
Is the story of my life with dad and me.

It Must Have Been Hard

It must have been hard to tell your son
You're not his father —no not the one,
Was nowhere around when he was conceived
Had nothing to do with what his mother believed.

It must have been hard to tell the lad
Who came for miles to see his dad
"Don't know why your mom would tell these lies;"
While you looked the child straight in the eyes.

It must have been hard to see this child
Walk away from you without a smile
Knowing the man he was leaving that day
Was still his father regardless of what he says.

Just think if the boy was really your son,
Then your joys for each other could have just begun;
But you turned him around-making him depart,
To a doubting father-it must have been hard.

When my father and my mother forsake
me, then the Lord will take me up.

Psalms 27:10

For I was my father's son, tender and only
beloved in the sight of my mother.

Proverbs 4:3

A father of the fatherless, and a judge of the
widows, is God in his holy habitation.

Psalms 68:5

It's Sad To Think

It's sad to think that a man like you
With all the things people think you can do
Could have planted a seed many years ago
And refused to watch that precious seed grow.

It's sad to think that you have a doubt
That the seed you planted is now your sprout;
Being blinded-you can't see the part of you
That took roots as the sprout grew and grew.

It's sad to think that your selfish greed
Makes you reject the sprout who you think has needs.
Not knowing that this sprout's only interest in you
Was to receive the love a sprout is due.

It's sad to think that at your gate
You rejected the sprout that was yours to cultivate
Saying you had no part in causing it to be.
That neglected sprout was me.

Part V

Marriage

Therefore shall a man leave his father and his mother, and shall cleave unto his wife: and they shall be one flesh

Genesis 2:24

Is It You

Is it you I waited so long to find
to open up this heart of mine
to give my love of never end
to be your warmth-your comforting friend?

Is it you with your gentle touch
could take so little and give so much
and turn my whole world anew
from clouds of gray to skies of blue?

Is it you that during my lonely hour
could make me blossom as a budding flower
creating the fragrance of joy of life
making my world a paradise?

Is it you my soul desperately desires
to send a mist to my heart that's now on fire
or wait for another promising to be true
originating the question, "Is it you?"

What True Lovers Do

Take of my hand sweet darling and let your anxiety pass,
For I give to you my life as long as it shall last.
Fret not what people say of me not loving you;
They don't know the meaning of love nor what true lovers do.

Never accept within your believing ears the lies that others say;
They wish our love to fall apart so they can make a play.
Doubt not my heavenly queen that my love for you is true,
For doubting lengthens the journey to what true lovers do.

If my heart another would win, to you I would confess,
But why would I settle for second choice when I already have the best.
You gave to me sweet enchantment and sparkled my world anew,
And together we found the secrets of what true lovers do.

Give me your trust, my precious, and I'll never let you down;
I'll shower you with affection-our love will jubilantly abound.
Climb aboard my cloud of love as we sail the skies of blue,
And then we'll continue the ecstasy of what true lovers do.

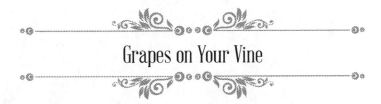

Grapes on Your Vine

Life may try to take my mind
Twist it and make me sway,
But the sweetest fruits are on your vine
So with you, my love, I stay.

Many grapes may look so sweet
Juicy and easy to find;
But still a grape I'm yet to eat,
That's sweeter than the grapes on your vine.

The sun shines bright on all the vines
The soil is rich as can be,
But I find your grapes are the only kind
That can truly satisfy me.

After your season has passed and gone
And the picking has all been done;
I will take and plant you in my home
And like in Spring-your vine can run.

You Believe In Me

There's no need to wonder if in my life there's another,
Just as long as we are in love with each other.
You give me no hassle if late I may be,
which reassures my faith that you believe in me.

Others tell you one day I will let you down,
And when needed most I will not be around.
You tell them our love is too deep for them to see;
In other words you're saying, you believe in me.

You show no doubts or fears in your eyes
Of whether I'm cheating or telling you lies;
You respect my decisions although you may disagree,
And tell me you're with me because you believe in me.

When things go wrong you make life worthwhile,
And when others would frown, you somehow smile.
You try not to cage me but allow me to be free,
And when others doubt, you believe in me.

We've Just Begun

When I thought we had reached
The zenith of our love affair
You proved to me that love has no limits;
Like a raging river-it goes on and on.

We have just begun to live;
Living the once impossible,
Sharing the unutterable,
And doing what was once unthinkable.

Each moment with you
Teaches a priceless lesson;
I learn how to be happy because
I learn how to be me.

Our love will forever grow-
Reaching for paradise.
We can sing a new song for
We've just begun.

What God Has Joined Together

It matters not what others say
or how they stare at you,
It matters not how long it takes
to make your dreams come true,
It matters not the time of day
the storm presented bad weather,
What matters most is never divide
what God has joined together.

It matters not your many friends
can turn their backs on you,
It matters not what you see in each other
is not what others may view,
It matters not your burdens are heavy
though once as light as a feather,
What matters is never put asunder
what God has joined together.

It matters not that bills are due
when funds have long been gone,
It matters not that sickness comes
and stays so very long,
It matters not that times are hard,
getting worse instead of better,
What matters most is never separate
what God has joined together.

Husband and Wife

Who is a husband and who is a wife?
They are two who swore to be together for life.
They are two who pledged until death do us part-
united forever with bonding of hearts.

Who is a husband and who is a wife?
They are two who stay joined through pleasure and strife.
They are two who are willing to forgive and forget-
wearied from their travel but gone too far to quit.

Who is a husband and who is a wife?
They are sacrificial beings for which to each other they sacrifice-
giving of self without bragging or boasting
and together claiming victory with laughter and toasting.

When two come together and jump over the broom,
find whenever conjoining is never too soon,
feel when being separated they lose meaning of life-
You now know the concept of husband and wife.

Part VI

Toils of Life

Mother's Body

Looking in her hands-what do I see,
Blisters of the first and second degree;
Scars from the heat of the hot summer sun,
Yet receiving only pennies for the work she's done.

Looking at her legs-what do I see,
Sore spots from the ankle up to the knee,
Spots from working in the early morning dews
Trying to make money to buy her children some shoes.

Looking at her hair-what do I see,
More gray strands than black but fresh as can be;
Gray from the years she grew wiser and older
As she carried the weight of her children on her shoulders.

Looking at her face-what do I see,
A smile that's pure and precious to me;
A smile that gave strength when I was weak,
For when the world was bitter her smile was sweet.

Looking at mother my eyes behold
A sweet, loving person more precious than gold;
One who will die for her children to live,
Who knows no taking, just knows how to give.

Favour is deceitful, and beauty is vain: but a woman that feareth the Lord, she shall be praised. Give her of the fruit of her hands; and let her own works praise her in the gates.

Proverbs 31:30-31

Be of good courage and he shall strengthen your heart, all ye that hope in the Lord.

Psalms 31:24

People Are Like Flowers

People are like flowers-
beautiful
When given proper attention
and care;
But if rejected too long-
wither and die.

Within every heart is
a rose,
Ready to blossom by
the sun of kindness;
Leaving its fragrance on
all who passes.

When the heart is met
by clouds of bitterness and resentment
It becomes disturbed-
filled with anger and hate;
Every rose has thorns.

Be patient during the storm
the sun will shine again.
Only the weak flowers die
after the storm has ended.

When thrown about by
the storm of life,
Everyone needs someone
to bring them closer together,
Or like flowers in an open field
They become wild.

Do The Best You Can

Don't try to understand everything that I do,
It's a far better thing to just understand you.
Don't accept my way as being the only way
For the world doesn't turn on what I say.

The world is not made to be ruled by one man
Each individual should carry the same weight in his hands.
The color of the skin shouldn't determine one's fate,
Nor should it bring one color love and the other hate.

The world should stop having big I's and little u's,
We all should have rewards and we all have some dues.
If every man would pay his debts to his nation
There would be a much peaceful and loving generation.

Sometimes our thoughts should stay at home plate
Instead of speaking foolish talk that the listener hates.
It is a far better skill to control the tongue
Than shift it in fourth gear and let it run.

Too many times we stand when we should be in our seats
And at times when we should stand, our legs become weak.
A man knows when to talk and when not to talk,
He knows when he should run and when he should just walk.

Knowing the thing to do and doing what you know
Requires a bit of wisdom that only a few show.
The kind of man who succeeds and appears to be a Super Man
Has learned that life gives to those who do the best they can.

God Still Loves You

When life seems empty because of pains of the day,
When all of your labor seems to go without pay,
When lies cloud your mind but you want to be true,
There's one good consolation-God still loves you.

When you're feeling kind of lonely and need a friend,
When the whirlwind of doubt is taking you for a spin,
When clouds of despair are blocking progressive view,
Find comfort in knowing that God still loves you.

When you make a mistake that you can't seem to forget,
When you're tired of failing but can't seem to quit,
When you're running low on patience and wondering what to do,
Always remember in your heart that God still loves you.

When you realize a change in your life must take place,
When you strive to advance but still lag in the race,
Don't think of self or what self wants to do,
Turn it over to the Master for God still loves you.

I'm Ashamed

I'm ashamed of the things I've done
I regret false words that were said
Each victory achieved turned out failure
Vanity had me mislead.

I'm ashamed of the thoughts inside
My ways of justification I disdain
I hate not doing that I should do
I abhor using righteousness for a game.

I'm ashamed of the pain I create
No joy can be found in my plight
It hurts when I think of rejecting the needy
I suffer for substituting wrong for right.

I'm ashamed for not loving the unlovable
Give to those who can give is my game
I suffer because of my selfishness and greed
But the pain comes from refusing to change.

Part VII

Friendship

When You Need a Friend

When you need a friend to share your load
And help make smooth your rugged road,
Just give me a call and I'll be there
To comfort, strengthen and show I care.

When you need a friend to relax your mind
Because peace seems so hard to find,
rest assured I'll be on my way-
Removing your clouds for a brighter day.

When you need a friend to be by your side,
Because you need to escape with no place to hide;
I'll provide for you a solitude
Where you may dwell when the world seems rude.

When you need a friend for no reason at all
or you feel your world is about to fall,
It matters not problems large or small
If you're ever in need, just call.

Little Whispers

Sitting in my easy chair with each thought gently on you;
Reminiscing of days gone by, enjoying the things we use to do.
Yet all that's left of you and me are sweet memories on my mind,
That somehow manages to slip out in little whispers sometimes.

Could it have been your touch that keeps you always near;
For when I'm sad and lonely, thoughts of you bring me cheer.
It could have been the joy and beauty of you being mine
That causes little whispers of you to slip out sometimes.

Somehow I'm never alone for I know you are there,
Resting easy in my heart-always seeming to care.
Now maybe it's not good to dream or talk while alone,
But little whispers of you are comfort when friends are gone.

No one can bring the past into the future again,
But I will keep you with me in memory as a friend.
Your love shall stay in my heart that I may be strong;
I'll speak to you in little whispers when I am all alone.

Showing Is Stronger Than Words

Why tell me-
You want and
Care for me too,
Showing those emotions
Will let me know
you do.

Darkness covered my life
Until you came along,
Still, I wasn't contented for
Only your words were strong.

Telling me your feelings
But not acting in accord
Only prove you are dealing
With words and not the heart.

Love runs deeper
Than the depths of the sea,
and
Your words without action
Don't mean a thing to me.

True love depends on deeds
and emotions,
Not on the things we say
or have heard,
The warmth that's given
Through trust and devotion
proves
Showing is stronger than words.

"You Gave"

You gave to me encouragement
To start me on my way,
And then you gave your smile
to brighten up my day.
I will treasure your warmth forever-
for as long as life shall last.
You didn't smother me with defeat
but made me feel head of the class.

You gave to me the will
to succeed regardless of odds,
and then you showed me the future
to level this rugged road I trod.
You made my journey seem smoother
though it may still be the same,
And may they place your name
in the teachers Hall of Fame

You gave to me a gift
that time could never take,
for you presented yourself as a friend
that only God could make.
You gave a lasting impression
with the positive words you said,
And smiled while giving me a second chance
when others would have frowned instead.

A Glow In You

Even though we traveled a different road
destiny brought us together,
And though there's confusion of kindred ties
I feel closer now than ever.
For we all are one big family
in search of what is true,
And when the light of justice seems dim
I see a glow in you.

Even though our paths are miles apart
and may never intersect,
there is a trail that branches off
from which our hearts connect.
And as we journey into the unknown
exchanging the old for the new
The way is made brighter each day
because of a glow in you.

For thou wilt light my candle: the Lord my God will enlighten my darkness.

Psalms 18:28

Printed in the United States
By Bookmasters